geisha™

geisha™

by
Andi Watson

book design by
Steven Birch @ Servo
front cover design by
Andi Watson

edited by
Jamie S. Rich

Published by Oni Press, Inc.
Joe Nozemack, publisher
Jamie S. Rich, editor in chief

additional editing
on original series by
Bob Schreck

*This collects issues 1-4
of the Oni Press comic
book* Geisha.

ONI PRESS, INC.
6336 SE Milwaukie Avenue
PMB30
Portland, OR 97202
USA

www.onipress.com

First edition: July 1999
ISBN 0-9667127-2-2

1 3 5 7 9 10 8 6 4 2
PRINTED IN CANADA.

introduction

by matt wagner

Okay, so I admit it.

At first, I thought he was a she.

My first exposure to Andi Watson's work was through his initial forays into the world of independent comics – a slow-but-surely evolving book known as *Skeleton Key*, published by my long-time pals at Slave Labor Graphics. I was immediately attracted to the book's quirky graphic design and what I perceived as a growing sense of well-honed focus. As with nearly all of us comic creators, the truly important lessons learned are to be found in what to leave out of our work. Andi's early drawing was crowded with superfluous nuggets of detail that you could visibly feel him letting go of from issue to issue. His cover work, more than anything else, exemplified his steadily growing powers of minimalism.

But, as stated above, my *other* initial reaction was, "Oh, great! Another female cartoonist!" We can always use more of *those* in this testosterone-laden industry. Apart from the distaff spelling of the artist's first name, this impression was strengthened by the delightful femininity of Andi's work. Rather than falling into the divisive two-camp system of most gal-comics (those being either scantily clad superhero wannababes or crudely drawn, pissed-off alternachicks), Andi's stories simply centered on the main character as...a girl. No obtrusive politics or seduction. No excessive agenda or estrogen. Simply a main character involved in a fantastic adventure – one who was female and came with the same feelings of wonder, anxiety, delight, and dismay as the rest of we penis-endowed humans. Holy shit, what a concept!

And then I learned how wrong I was.

It was several years later that my more recent pals at Oni Press showed me the cover (along with a small promotional folder) of Andi's latest offering – *Geisha*. I remember being even more impressed with the direction and style of this title. Andi had at last succeeded in refining the many disparate influences in his art into a unified whole that was utterly his own (more on that in a moment). Luckily, before I could blurt out, "Wow! So this is by the gal that does *Skeleton Key*?" one of the Oni-ites said, "Yeah, he's got this planned as a four-issue series, and it reads just great!"

He? *Andi* is a he?

Which impressed me even more. For all the focus on the female lead in his stories, Andi never sacrifices the male element. In *Geisha*, the main character's brother, Cherry, is every bit as flawed, likeable, and humane as his sister Jomi (aaaaaand visually based on Mike Ness from Social Distortion, one of the most utterly macho bands around). That balancing act is a hard one to maintain, and Andi nimbly straddles the line without ever slipping into caricature above character. To Andi, it's neither a man's world nor a woman's – it's the human drama that truly matters. Even if your title character happens to be an android, as well.

Which is another clever weaving of Andi's. By titling his book *Geisha* and then making it noticeably devoid of the immediate Western image that leaps to mind – that of a delicate, kimonoed courtesan – he forces us to address the word in its literal translation as "art person." Thus, Jomi's status as a manufactured life form is an analogy of the alienation she feels from her artistic longings rather than from the fact that she is a girl. In fact, physically, she's one of the toughest characters in the book, shrugging off thugs and bullets far easier than the crass assessments of her harshest critic. Her feelings of anxiety over what to create and how to create it beautifully exemplify the dilemmas of human endeavor. What a subtle and difficult emotion to get across--not to mention it

being woven into the subtext of an exciting story, as well.

Additionally, the title works as a metaphor for the creator himself. As I said, it's obvious that Andi appreciates and draws inspiration from a wide variety of sources. One of the obvious roots to his approach is, of course, Japanese manga. Yet, somehow, Andi manages to escape the "sameness" that plagues so many purveyors of this style. Incredibly, he has somehow melded the childish immediacy of the manga look with the highly sophisticated brevity of the *New Yorker* school of cartooning. And all the while, his characters speak about the finer points of art restoration, technical forgeries, and critical acclaim – in-between bouts of cracking crimes, exposing corporate corruption, and fighting giant robots. With his covers inspired by a wide range of artistic masters and a story line that could never have been written by anyone else, Andi Watson has made a wonderful leap into that golden stage that is every creator's dream (in many ways, Jomi's growth herein reflects his own) – the formation of a unique and realized voice.

He truly is...a geisha.

MATT WAGNER
May, 1999

Matt Wagner is one of the pioneering creators who made independent comics a major creative and commercial force in the '80s and '90s. Both of his main series, Mage: The Hero Discovered *and* Grendel, *as well as his work on* Batman *and* The Demon, *are considered touchstones in the industry. He is currently finishing* Mage II: The Hero Defined, *the long-awaited sequel to* Mage.

Chapter: one

Chapter: two

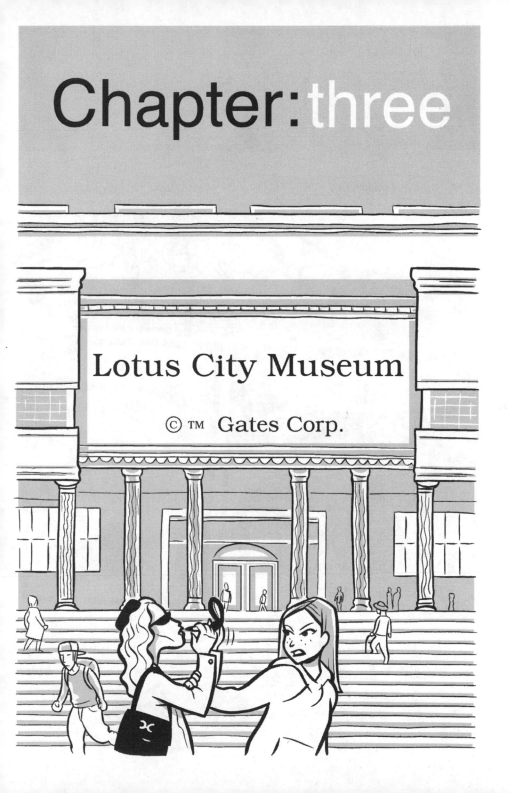

Chapter:four

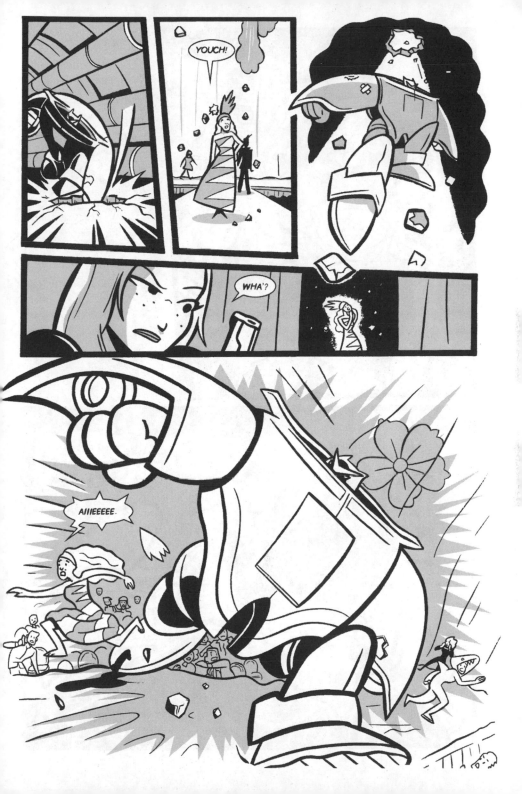

gallery

The following pages contain studies of classic paintings that Andi did to prepare himself for the Geisha series.

Original cover design for Geisha #1, back when it went by its original title, The Minx (which was changed due to a similarly titled comic from a competing publisher).

Andi's proposal for Geisha *contained the first sixteen pages of #1, which he later redrew for the actual comic. Some of those original pages are shown here for the first time.*

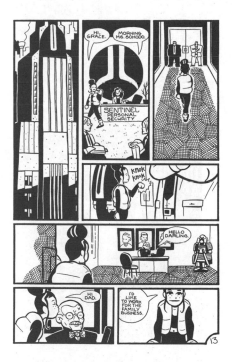